WONDER-WORKERS!

WONDER-WORKERS!

How They Perform The Impossible

JOE NICKELL

Prometheus Books • Buffalo, New York

Published 1991 by Prometheus Books

95 94 93 92 91   5 4 3 2 1

Library of Congress Cataloging-in-Publication Data

Nickell, Joe.
    Wonder-workers! : how they perform the impossible / Joe Nickell ; with illustrations by the author.
        p.   cm.
    Includes bibliographical references.
    Summary: Biographies of apparent wonder-workers, some of whom were masters of illusion and some of whom actually claimed to have psychic powers, including Daniel Home, Harry Houdini, and Edgar Cayce.
    ISBN 0-87975-688-8
    1. Magicians—Biography—Juvenile literature. 2. Psychics—Biography—Juvenile literature. 3. Entertainers—Biography—Juvenile literature. [1. Magicians. 2. Psychics. 3. Entertainers.] I. Title.
GV1545.A2N53   1991
793.8′092′2—dc20
[B]   91-27484
                                                                              CIP
                                                                               AC

Printed in the United States of America on acid-free paper.

In Memory of My Father,
J. Wendell Nickell,
Magician

Contents

Introduction

I have always been fascinated by wonder-workers—people who seem to have special powers, the apparent ability to accomplish the impossible.

As a result, before becoming a private detective and then an investigative writer, I studied conjuring (stage magic) and became a professional stage magician. That is, for a few years—either as a magician, a magic clown, or sometimes a mentalist (a conjurer who performs "mind reading" and similar tricks)—I *became* a wonder-worker.

In addition to my fellow conjurers and mentalists, I came to know such other wonder-workers as escape artists ("The Amazing Randi," for example), fire-eaters and fire-breathers (like "El Diablo the Human Volcano"), and others who seemed to have magical abilities.

I soon realized that, just as conjurers use magic tricks to work their special wonders, so do many other people who appear to have magical powers. For example, "Atasha the Gorilla Girl," a sideshow attraction at a carnival where I worked, did not really change from a beautiful young woman into an ape, although she certainly appeared to. Instead the transformation was a trick using a mirror, special lighting, and another person wearing a gorilla suit.

But not all wonder-workers are tricksters. Some rely on special knowledge, skills, or scientific principles to help them work their seeming wonders. For instance, sword swallowers do actually swallow swords, a very dangerous stunt, but they first learn to conquer the gag reflex (the impulse to retch when something is stuck down the throat). Then follows a long period of careful practice, beginning with shorter blades and working up to longer ones. Naturally, an untrained person would risk serious harm—even death—attempting such a feat.

In this book are stories about ten famous wonder-workers: men and women who were seemingly fireproof, able to walk through solid walls, capable of interacting with spirits of the dead, or of foretelling the future, or who otherwise appeared to accomplish the impossible.

We will look at each in the way that paranormal investigators (or "magic detectives") do. That is, we will examine their claims in the spirit of scientific inquiry to learn whether or not they did have paranormal powers—powers beyond the range of nature and normal human experience.

From such examinations we can learn more about our world and our place in it. We can also experience the thrill of adventure as we travel into the incredible realms of the wonder-workers.

"THE FIRE KING"

Ivan Chabert

So-called "fire-eaters" of one sort or another have performed since ancient times. But Ivan Chabert (pronounced e-VAHN shuh-BEAR) was known as the French "Incombustible Phenomenon"—that is, one who was actually *fireproof!*

Like other such performers before him, Chabert (1792–1859) could eat fiery coals and sip blazing oil. But his greatest feat was stepping into a burning oven carrying raw meat, and—after several suspense-filled minutes—emerging unharmed with the meat fully cooked.

One of the earliest of the fire-eating wonder-workers lived in ancient Roman times. He was a Syrian called Eunus (d. 133 B.C.). In order to excite his fellow slaves to revolt against the Romans, Eunus claimed he had received supernatural powers from the gods who foretold he would someday be king. As proof, Eunus exhaled jets of fire, just like the legendary dragon.

However, a writer named Florus was skeptical and guessed the secret of Eunus's fire-breathing trick. Florus stated that Eunus hid a nutshell in his mouth that contained burning material. The shell had a small opening at each end so that, when the fake wizard blew through it, sparks and flames were projected. (At first Eunus's rebellion was successful and he named himself King Antiochus. But soon the Romans regained control and Eunus was captured, later dying in prison.)

In seventeenth-century England, a fire-eater named Richardson appeared to dine on various fiery materials. He munched glowing coals, drank flaming liquids, and otherwise attempted to prove he was unharmed by fire.

In the eighteenth century a fire-eater named Robert Powell performed similar stunts at British fairs. And in the first part of the next century an Italian woman, Signora Josephine Giardelli, was exhibited in London as "The Fireproof Female." It was advertised that

> She will, without the least symptoms of pain, put boiling melted lead in her mouth, and emit the same with the imprint of her teeth thereon; red-hot irons will be passed over various parts of her body; she will walk over a bar of red-hot iron with her naked feet; will . . . put boiling oil in her mouth!

She was rivaled by Chabert who arrived in London in 1818, his posters proclaiming him "The Fire King." He too ate burning materials. As *The Times* reported in 1826:

> . . . he refreshed himself with a hearty meal of phosphorus . . . he washed down this infernal fare with solutions of arsenic and oxalic acid . . . he next swallowed . . . several spoonsful of boiling oil and, as a dessert . . . , helped himself with his naked hand to a considerable quantity of molten lead . . . the exhibitor offered to swallow Prussic acid, perhaps the most powerful of known poisons, if any good-natured person could furnish him with a quantity of it.

But it was Chabert's feat of the fiery oven that created the greatest sensation. He entered the oven, actually an iron chest about six by seven feet, which had been heated to some 600 degrees Fahrenheit, carrying a thick steak and a leg of lamb. Closing the doors behind him, he remained there, talking with the audience through a tin tube, while the meat cooked. Then he flung open the doors and stepped out in triumph.

As you may have guessed, Monsieur Chabert was no more fireproof than other such performers. He merely used magic tricks and simple scientific principles to create that illusion. For example, as the magician and writer Walter Gibson explained:

> When he "swallows" burning oil, the performer does not ladle up liquid, but merely lets the spoon become wet. The few drops that adhere will burn for a moment, giving him time to raise the spoon to his mouth. Then he exhales, extinguishing the flame, and immediately takes the spoon in his mouth, as though swallowing the oil.

Also,

> Chewing of molten metals until they become solid is accomplished by using an alloy of bismuth, lead and block tin, which has a very low melting point. It is dropped upon the moist tongue where it will harden without burning and becomes a solid lump.

Although placing a torch in the mouth would be disastrous for the average person, the fire-eater has expert training and knowledge. He uses specially prepared torches, keeps his mouth well filled with saliva, and tips his head back; then he *exhales* as the flame enters his mouth, which is then quickly closed. Deprived of oxygen, the flame goes out almost immediately.

Some performers attempt to prove their resistance to fire by walking barefoot across red-hot embers. This is possible because wood does not conduct heat well and because the time of contact is kept quite brief. (Experiments show that it is possible to make a short walk across hot coals or a longer walk over cooler embers. As most people know, one can pass a finger quickly through a candle flame, but drawing the finger slowly through the flame would result in burns.)

But what about Chabert's withstanding the ordeal of the burning oven? Was that just a trick, too?

It was indeed. In fact Chabert was caught in one deception: placing the thermometer in the fire to give the impression the oven was very hot. Actually the temperature was just above 200 degrees. And, because heat rises, the lower portion of the oven remained relatively cool.

The fire was lit in the center of the large iron box and Chabert was able to lie safely on the floor by the doors, his head covered by a protective hood. He could breathe, of course, through the speaking tube.

So that the meat would cook quickly, Chabert hung it on hooks directly over the fire! When it was done, he made his dramatic exit from the oven.

In 1830, however, Chabert made a mistake, underestimating the British fondness for animals. He performed a trick involving two dogs and the deadly poison, prussic acid. He appeared to give both animals the poison, allowing one to die to demonstrate the acid's potency, then saved the other, supposedly by administering a magical potion he had invented.

Londoners were less impressed by his saving the one dog than they were the senseless death of the other, and Chabert's popularity diminished. Before long, he left England for America.

There Chabert continued his career and gave successful performances in New York City. He was less appreciated elsewhere, however, and soon found himself in financial trouble.

Chabert quit the stage and opened up an apothecary shop (drugstore) on Grand Street in New York. Using the name "J. Xavier Chabert, MD," he began selling quack medicines. He peddled something called a "Chinese Lotion" and even sold an elixir that was supposed to cure tuberculosis.

Unfortunately, the elixir did not work. Doubly unfortunately, Chabert contracted the disease himself and, on August 28, 1859, he died.

Today, mostly in carnival sideshows, one may still see a fire-eater or "fire-breather" (one who sips a flammable liquid and blows it across a flame to create great bursts of fire). But none seems to work such wonders as did Ivan Chabert, "The Fire King."

Selected Sources

Christopher, Milbourne. *Panorama of Magic* (New York: Dover, 1962), pp. 2, 36–40.
Dawes, Edwin A. *The Great Illusionists* (Secaucus, N.J.: Chartwell Books, 1979), pp. 57–60.
"Eunus," *Encyclopaedia Britannica,* 1960, vol. 8, p. 814.
Gibson, Walter. *Secrets of Magic: Ancient and Modern* (New York: Grosset & Dunlap, 1967), pp. 41–43.

"MONARCH OF MAGICIANS"

Robert-Houdin

One of history's greatest conjurers, called "the father of modern magic," once made clocks for a living.

Born Jean Eugene Robert (pronounced ro-BEAR) in the town of Blois in 1805, he was the son of a humble French watchmaker. Although the youth wished to pursue the family trade, his father wanted better things for his son. After sending him to school until the age of eighteen, he encouraged him to become a solicitor (a type of lawyer).

With his skilled hands, which produced excellent penmanship, Jean Robert easily got a job as a clerk in a law office. From morning until night he penned copies of legal documents.

His thoughts, though, were elsewhere, and early each morning, before his father arose, the young man slipped into his workshop. There he tinkered with the watchmaker's tools, making clever clockwork devices.

He copied one mechanical device that had been given to his father to repair. It was a small box whose top represented an outdoor scene. Pressing a button caused a tiny rabbit to appear and run across the landscape, followed by a little hunter and his miniature dog. When the hunter fired his gun, the device made a suitable noise, whereupon the rabbit disappeared into a thicket.

Even with today's sophisticated computer toys, we can appreciate the skill that went into making such a little mechanism by hand. Of course, Jean Robert's father was impressed when he was shown the finished product, but he still encouraged his son to pursue legal training.

Soon, the young man got a job as an advanced law clerk. This gave him more free time, which he spent making more ingenious mechanisms. The office contained a large cage with canaries that caught his imagination, and he began to outfit the cage with various clever devices: a trick perch, little baths with tiny pumps to fill them, and so on.

However, as he would later write, "The pleasure I felt in carrying out these small schemes soon made me forget I was in a lawyer's office for any other purpose than to be at the beck and call of canaries." Eventually, though, his employer chastised him for playing at work.

Yet, seeing how talented the boy was and how much he wished to make unique mechanisms, the lawyer talked with Jean's father on his behalf. Finally, the father agreed that his son should take up the family trade.

At last, Jean was seriously learning the curious workings of clocks and similar mechanisms. One evening he went to a bookseller's shop to purchase a two-volume work titled *Treatise on Clockmaking*. In his haste, however, the shopkeeper mistook one of the volumes, and Jean found himself reading a book on magic tricks.

Now another world was presented to Jean Robert's eager mind. He began to learn the secrets of magicians. His dexterity, or manual skill, made him good at "sleight of hand" tricks, tricks accomplished by the clever handling of objects. (For example, we have all seen magicians cause coins or balls or cards to appear and disappear at their fingertips. That is done by slight of hand.)

Jean even paid a local man to teach him the art of juggling, and he practiced juggling balls in the air while reading his books, which helped improve his dexterity.

Quickly, Jean progressed in learning his trade, and he then went to work as a repairman in a master watchmaker's shop. But soon the lure of magic called him.

He later claimed in his *Memoirs* that he spent several months in the company of a traveling magician named Torrini. (Actually, since there is no proof such a magician existed, some people think that this part was added to make the *Memoirs* more interesting.)

Torrini, we are told, traveled by wagon—a unique wagon. Already large, it could be extended, like a telescope, to twice its length. It thus served as a compact theater, complete with a little stage lit by candles.

Torrini performed a variety of standard magicians' effects, but he was especially skillful at sleight-of-hand tricks with playing cards. Like many such conjurers, he also exhibited clockwork robots called *automata* (aw-TOM-uh-tuh). Torrini's automaton was a sort of jack-in-the-box figure that performed some antics before returning to the box. It was in bad condition, however, and Jean set to work to repair it.

After many adventures, young Jean Robert returned home. At a party he met his future wife, pretty seventeen-year-old Josephe Cecile Eglantine Houdin. After their marriage in 1830 he added her last name to his own, thereafter being known as Robert-Houdin (pronounced ro-BEAR-hoo-DAN).

His wife's father was, interestingly enough, owner of a clock business in Paris. Monsieur Houdin sold clocks wholesale and also made special scientific clocks and other mechanisms. Quite naturally, he helped his new son-in-law set up his own business.

While Robert-Houdin repaired watches, he expanded his business by creating clever mechanisms. He invented an "alarm light"—an alarm clock that sounded at the desired time and also produced a lighted candle! He also made mechanical toys, including a little wind-up magician, a dancer on a tightrope, and singing birds.

While he worked hard at his business (so hard that he actually fell ill for a time) Robert-Houdin longed to become a great magician. He discovered a little shop that sold magic equipment, and he bought several items. He visited the performances of conjurers who appeared in Paris theaters. He also began to design and make magical automata.

His two skills, magic and mechanics, were united in one clever creation. This was a "Mysterious Clock" that had a transparent dial and stand, which, therefore, seemed to operate without any mechanism. Of course, this was just a magician's illusion, the clockworks being cleverly hidden.

He now seriously planned his career as a magician and set to work to create his very own theater for that purpose.

Obtaining a loan from a friend, a French count, Robert Houdin rented an upstairs room in a suitable building. He hired an architect to draw up the necessary plans for transforming it into a small performance hall. Then he hired carpenters and other workmen to carry out the necessary tasks.

At eight o'clock on the evening of July 13, 1845, Robert Houdin's "Des Soirees Fantastiques" began. (A soiree is an evening party.) Of course it was a fantastical evening, promising—according to the playbills advertising the show—"AUTOMATA, SLEIGHT OF HAND, MAGIC."

Although understandably nervous, the forty-year-old Frenchman ordered the curtains to be raised and then walked boldly on stage.

Robert-Houdin did sleight-of-hand tricks with playing cards and performed other magical feats, including one of his favorites called "the surprising pocket-handkerchief." Borrowing a handkerchief from a spectator, he produced from it an amazing variety of objects: sugar plums, feathers and fans, and, finally, an entire basket of flowers!

His magical automata included "The Orange Tree," which blossomed as if by magic. A pass of his magician's wand transformed the blossoms into fruit. He tossed the oranges—real oranges!—one by one into the audience. Then two mechanical butterflies suddenly appeared and fluttered over the tree.

Another automaton was "The Pastry-Cook." A miniature chef appeared in the doorway of a little pastry shop, which was about the size of a dollhouse. At the spectators' requests, the chef dashed into the shop and brought forth cakes, buns, and other pastries. Only part of this feat was accomplished by mechanical means, however: The magician's little boy was hidden inside the shop! He filled the pastry cook's arms with the requested item.

Robert-Houdin's later shows produced even more amazing feats. His "Ethereal Suspension" was an illusion in which the magician's son was balanced on a cane, seemingly overcoming the force of gravity. (The actual means of support is cleverly hidden, and the method is one magicians naturally wish to keep a secret!)

In his "Second Sight" trick, Robert-Houdin's son was blindfolded, yet he could accurately describe any object—a coin, handkerchief, pipe, or whatever—that a spectator submitted. (His father had a means of giving the information to his son, unknown to the audience.)

As word of such wonderful illusions spread, audiences flocked to the theater. Robert-Houdin soon went abroad, giving tours elsewhere in Europe and in the British Isles. Over the years, he appeared three times before England's Queen Victoria.

Eventually he turned over his theater to a pupil and retired to his country estate at Blois. Naturally, his house was outfitted with ingenious devices: an electrical fire alarm that was set off by a rise in temperature, a burglar alarm system, and other such wonders. In the stables, horses were fed on schedule by a clock-operated mechanism.

During his retirement Robert-Houdin devoted his time to further electrical research and invention. His electric clock won him a gold medal in 1855. He also devised a battery-powered mantelpiece clock and many other inventions.

In 1856, Robert-Houdin came out of retirement briefly. At the request of the French government he went on a mission to Algeria. There, alleged Arab miracle-workers were encouraging the tribes to revolt against French rule.

The French conjurer was advertised as a great sorcerer, and many of the native chieftains were summoned to view his performance. In addition to feats of sleight of hand, Robert-Houdin exhibited a box that he could pick up easily but that an Arab strongman was powerless to lift.

He also demonstrated a death-defying feat: a pistol was loaded with a marked lead ball and fired at an apple that the Frenchman held before his heart. The bullet, positively identified by its marking, safely lodged in the apple!

To accomplish the first trick, Robert-Houdin used an electrically operated magnet to secure the box. And he employed a sleight-of-hand trick with the bullet. (He probably switched a harmless wax bullet for the lead one, then secretly pushed the marked bullet into the apple.)

As a result of his performance, the Arab wonder-workers were outdone. The rebellion was stopped. The chieftains presented Robert-Houdin with a scroll that honored him, a scroll still kept by his descendants.

In 1871, at the age of 65, the great magician—the first truly modern one—died of pneumonia. Although he had been a professional trickster, he used his illusions and deceptions, as well as his wonderful inventions, only for good.

Selected Sources

Christopher, Milbourne. *Panorama of Magic.* New York: Dover Publications, 1962, pp. 72–79.

Dawes, Edwin A. *The Great Illusionists.* Secaucus, N.J.: Chartwell Books, 1979, pp. 121–127.

Wraxall, Lascelles, translator. *Memoirs of Robert-Houdin,* with introduction and notes by Milbourne Christopher. New York: Dover Publications, 1964.

SORCERER AMONG THE SPIRITS

Daniel Home

Unlike Robert-Houdin, who was an admitted trickster, Daniel Home (pronounced HUME) claimed he really had a sorcerer's powers. Supposedly, he not only could levitate (that is, float in the air), but he could perform other wonders—even communicate with the dead!

He was born on March 20, 1833, in Currie, a small town near Edinburgh, Scotland. Daniel's parents were William and Elizabeth (Macneil) Home. The family was a large but unhappy one, Daniel's father being an alcoholic who mistreated the boy's mother. Because of this, when Daniel was only a year old, he was adopted by an aunt who had no children of her own.

At the age of nine, Daniel's adoptive parents moved to America. There, at the age of seventeen, he became attracted to mystical phenomena, particularly spiritualism. He performed in New England, and later (1855) he sailed to England. There, and in other European countries, he worked his spiritualistic wonders.

Spiritualism is a belief that "spirits of the dead" communicate with living people. Modern Spiritualism began in 1848 at Hydesville, New York, with two young girls, Margaret and Katherine Fox. Mysterious rapping sounds came from the girls' room, even though they appeared to be asleep. The strange knocks seemed to prove a story that the house was haunted.

Soon the Fox sisters were communicating with the "ghost." He would answer their questions by knocking a certain number of times to indicate *yes* or *no* or to give other answers. Before long the girls were able to communicate with additional spirits, and they traveled across the United States with an older sister promoting their "Spiritualist society."

Some people, however, were skeptical (doubtful) of the alleged spirit communications. They thought the rapping sounds came from beneath a table where Margaret was sitting. When they controlled her feet, the noises stopped.

Years later Margaret confessed that she had produced the sounds herself. She was able to slip off her shoe and snap her big toe against the bare floor to produce the knocking sounds! While her sister (who had participated in the deception) looked on, Margaret gave a public demonstration of her method. Her explanation was verified by doctors.

In the meantime, Spiritualism flourished, becoming a widespread fad. People calling themselves "mediums" pretended to contact the spirits of people's dead relatives. In dark rooms, mediums held sessions called séances (SAY-ahn-sez) where the sitters typically held hands around a table.

Spirits might be seen as glowing shapes moving eerily about the room, or they might make their presence known in other ways, such as by producing "apports." These were flowers or other objects that would mysteriously appear at the séance table. Often the medium would go into a "trance" and then speak as if the spirits were talking through him or her.

These effects could easily be produced by trickery. Ghostly forms were often created by waving about a piece of cloth that was specially treated so that it glowed in the dark. The apports could be concealed in the medium's clothes or elsewhere (perhaps in a secret compartment in a chair) until needed.

The trances would be especially convincing if the spiritualist had time to conduct secret research on the sitters before the séance. The information thus obtained would then be given out as if it were provided by the spirits.

Sometimes mediums produced more elaborate "materializations" of spirits. The medium's assistants would dress in costumes complete with fake beards and wigs. They would then slip into the darkened room by means of trap doors or secret panels and pretend to be ghosts. Many people were willing to pay large sums of money to supposedly communicate with their deceased loved ones.

"Spirit photography" was also practiced. In the 1860s, a Boston photographer named William H. Mumler produced photos in which ghostly forms were included in his sitters' portraits. His deception was uncovered, however, when some of the "spirits" were recognized as living Boston residents! Such photographs were easily made by a variety of techniques, and fake spirit pictures have continued to be made in modern times.

It was in this climate of widespread fakery that Daniel Home flourished. He added a middle name, "Dunglas," to give a false connection to an earlier Lord Dunglas and thereby seem to be of noble birth. He then set out on a life of ease.

Although he did not actually charge a fee, Home took advantage of his hosts who were often wealthy aristocrats. In hopes of witnessing some of his marvels, they eagerly paid his expenses and showered him with gifts.

In one instance, when some admirers in Italy intended to present him with a coat, Home ordered an expensive one and then slipped away with the money, so that his friends had to pay the bill twice. He thus earned a bad reputation among some people, but others were deceived by his charm and by his apparent wonder-workings.

For example, Home attempted to prove he was fireproof (although his demonstrations were nothing compared to those of "The

Fire King," *see p. 13*), and he performed other magical feats, including spiritualistic phenomena.

Often during his séances ghostly hands would appear. They would ring bells placed beneath a table, tug at ladies' dresses, and perform similar pranks. When he was once asked why the effects usually occurred *beneath* the table, Home replied that people's doubts and disbelief had a negative effect on the spirits' work. Skeptics, of course, thought he was just making excuses to conceal his trickery.

On one occasion when he was staying with a wealthy solicitor, Home met the famous poets Robert and Elizabeth Barrett Browning. That evening during a séance in a dimly lit room, a "spirit" hand placed a wreath on Mrs. Browning's head. At first deceived, she later agreed with her husband that the hand had slipped from beneath the table and that Home had played a trick. Ever afterward Robert Browning referred to the medium with contempt and called him a scoundrel.

Home's greatest power, however, was supposedly that of levitation. That alleged phenomenon has a long history. Ancient legends of saints and mystics who could float in the air appear, however, to be only that: legends.

Fakirs (or mystics) from India were also supposedly able to self-levitate. When the fakirs came to London in the 1930s, the feat was photographed and magicians confirmed how the trick was done. The fakirs were merely performing a suspension illusion like that of Robert-Houdin.

Stage magicians do create the effect of levitation with their "Floating Lady" illusion. A hoop is even passed over the lady's body so as to prove, supposedly, that there are no hidden wires or supports. Nevertheless, it is just a magicians' trick. (It is explained in Walter Gibson's *Secrets of Magic Ancient and Modern.* See the list of sources at the end of this chapter.)

One thing seems certain: Under controlled conditions and surrounded by expert magicians, no one today is able to levitate. Was Daniel Home a unique exception, or was his feat, too, a trick?

On one occasion in 1852, when Home was nineteen, he floated so high that his head touched the ceiling. One spectator who had been holding his hand felt his feet and noted that they were well off the floor. Home indicated a spirit lifted him.

Remember that this took place in complete darkness, where trickery would be easy. As magician Milbourne Christopher writes:

> One method used then, and later, by mediums is most convincing. In the dark the psychic slips off his shoes as he tells the sitters his body is becoming weightless. The sitter to the medium's left grasps his left hand, the one to the right puts a hand on the mystic's shoes, near the toes. Holding his shoes together with his right hand pressing the inner sides, the medium slowly raises them in the air as he first squats then stands on his chair. The man holding his hand reports the medium is ascending; so does the sitter who touches the shoes. Until I tried this myself, it was hard to believe that spectators in a dark room could be convinced an ascension was being made.

On another occasion, at a house in London in 1868, Home reportedly floated out one upstairs window and glided through another into an adjacent room! Although the rooms were dark, three men claimed to have witnessed the feat by moonlight. Unfortunately, an 1868 almanac shows that there would have been a new moon. According to historian Trevor Hall the moon "therefore could not even faintly have illuminated the room."

Also, the three witnesses gave different versions of what actually happened. No one actually *saw* Home floating outside the window. All we really know is that they were *told* he went out the one window and then saw him *appear* to come in the other.

The great magician Houdini thought Home might secretly have had a wire dangling outside which he used to swing from one window balcony to the other. Another researcher thought a plank could have been placed between the balconies and that Home could have crawled across it.

Trevor Hall mentions an architect who carefully studied a photograph of the outside of the building. Hall believes the balconies were close enough (about four feet) that a person who was unafraid of heights could simply have stepped from one to the other.

Still other researchers have suggested that—after noisily opening the first window—Home slipped quietly in the dark to the other which he then opened and pretended to enter. It would have been difficult to tell whether his dimly silhouetted form was actually outside or inside the window. And people often "see" what they expect to see.

Whatever actually happened, the dark room and other circumstances suggest trickery. Home specifically instructed the witnesses to remain seated. "On no account leave your places," he insisted. What did he have to fear from their moving about? Probably he was afraid they might see how the trick was done!

In some séances, Home communicated advice from the "spirits" to those suffering from various ailments. However, the spirits were apparently unable to help cure his own tuberculosis. On June 21, 1886, at the age of fifty-three, he died of that disease.

His second wife attempted to enhance his memory by writing two books and getting a fountain built as a memorial. A much less favorable view of Home was expressed by the scientist, Sir David Brewster:

> Were Mr. Home to assume the character of Wizard of the West, I would enjoy his exhibition as much as that of other conjurers; but when he pretends to possess the power of introducing among the feet of his audience the spirits of the dead, bringing them into physical communication with their dearest relatives, and of revealing the secrets of the grave, he insults religion and common sense, and tampers with the most sacred feelings of his victims.

Selected Sources

Christopher, Milbourne. *ESP, Seers and Psychics* (New York: Thomas Y. Crowell, 1970), pp. 174–187.

Gibson, Walter. *Secrets of Magic: Ancient and Modern* (New York:

Grosset & Dunlap, 1967), pp. 81, 114–116.

Hall, Trevor H. *The Enigma of Daniel Home* (Buffalo: Prometheus Books, 1984).

Mulholland, John. *Beware Familiar Spirits* (1938; Reprinted, New York: Scribner, 1979).

THE HUMAN MAGNET

Lulu Hurst

In August 1883 at Cedarville, Georgia, there were disturbances in the home of the Hurst family. In the presence of their fifteen-year-old daughter, Lulu, small objects moved, crockery was smashed, popping sounds were heard, and other disturbances took place. It was as if Lulu's body had a magnet's power to attract or repel!

Certainly she could attract audiences: soon, known as the "Georgia Magnet," Lulu was packing lecture halls and opera houses in Atlanta, New York, Chicago, Milwaukee, and elsewhere. Crowds came to witness her apparent power.

In one demonstration, despite the efforts of several people to resist her, she could push them about the stage. Two strong men pressing against a stick she held out were unable to move her from where she stood. And holding a stick vertically, a man would attempt to push it down to the floor, but the alleged human magnet merely pressed her hand against the stick and prevented the action. The man seemed paralyzed by some mysterious force.

Did the teenage girl really have a magical power—a "Great Unknown," as she termed it—or was there some other explanation for her apparent wonders? Let's take a closer look.

The disturbances that began in the Hurst home were what today would be called "poltergeist" (POLE-ter-guyst) phenomena. Poltergeist is a German word meaning "noisy spirit."

Broken dishes and other damage was typical. Another effect—curious rapping sounds—reminded one of the Fox sisters (*see p. 28*). While the Fox sisters' "spirit" knocked in response to questions, Lulu's "unseen force" was musically inclined. For instance, if Lulu thought of some tune while she was lying in bed, it would be heard in rapping sounds coming from the bed's wooden frame.

Typically, when such disturbances are investigated by professional magicians or other knowledgeable persons, they turn out to be the result of juvenile pranks. Such was the case, we remember, with the Fox sisters' "spirit" rappings.

An earlier example took place in Newbury, Massachusetts, in 1679. Events attributed to a "demon" occurred at the home of a man named William Morse. Morse's grandson experienced strange behavior, such as shaking or clucking like a chicken. Objects were thrown about. And at night, as the grandparents and boy lay together in the same large bed, they were jabbed by sharp objects.

Then a visiting sailor told Mr. Morse that if he could spend a day with the boy the disturbances would end. Although there is no record of exactly what the sailor did, the devilish acts ceased. Apparently, the seaman simply counseled the boy about his mischief.

A similar case took place in England in 1772. Strange happenings began in the home of an elderly widow. Dishes and mirrors were broken. A clock and a lantern fell. So did a side of bacon and two hams that hung on hooks by the chimney. An egg flew through the air and broke on a cat's head. Water began to boil in a pail although it was away from the stove.

The disturbances centered around a young maid. She later confessed to a clergyman that she had been the "unseen force." She had thrown the egg at the cat. She placed a chemical in the pail to make the water bubble. She hung the slabs of meat so that their weight would cause the hooks to tear through their skins. Objects were moved when she secretly pulled a thin, almost invisible wire (or sometimes a long horsehair) attached to them.

More modern examples yield similar explanations. For instance, in Alabama, in 1959 a series of strange household fires was traced to a nine-year-old boy. He had wanted to cause his family to return to a city they used to live in.

In another case, in 1974, numerous poltergeist-type disturbances puzzled many people but eventually pointed to a thirteen-year-old girl. Finally, she was seen deliberately kicking one object, then she claim the poltergeist had moved it. The girl was said to have "deep hostilities" that resulted in her bad behavior.

In light of such cases, the "poltergeist" activity in Lulu Hurst's home seems likely to have been trickery that she was responsible for. But what about her "human magnet" demonstrations? These were even performed before scientists.

In Washington, D.C., a group of scientists examined Lulu. To determine if her power might be a form of electricity, they placed her on an insulated glass platform, but her powers seemed to continue as before.

Her successful performances began to make Lulu wealthy. So did use of her name in promoting such products as soap and cigars. One manufacturer of plows advertised that his product was as "strong as Lulu Hurst."

At the same time, there were problems. Spiritualists, followers of the Fox sisters, were claiming Lulu as one of their own, and this brought protests from ministers and other critics of Spiritualism. There were also other problems, as we shall see.

Writer Frank Edwards speaks of Lulu's "triumph in New York," claiming that when she appeared at Wallack's Theater, "the New York newspapers sang her praises." Actually, the *New York Times* of July 13, 1884, stated critically:

The "Phenomenon of the Nineteenth Century," which may be seen nightly at Wallack's, is not so much the famous Georgia

girl, with her mysterious muscle, as it is the audience which
gathers to wonder at her performance. It is a phenomenon of
stupidity, and it only goes to show how willingly people will
be fooled. . . .

The *Times* went on to describe Lulu's performance, which went
rather badly. A man named Thomas Johnson had apparently discovered her secret: In all the "tests" in which he was permitted to
take part, Mr. Johnson triumphed over the power—or "Great Unknown"—of Miss Hurst.

But just what was the Georgia girl's secret? As it happens, she
herself soon confessed it. This came after two years of performing,
when Lulu Hurst suddenly announced to reporters that she was giving
up her act. Having married the young man who managed her show,
she was returning home for the quiet life of a housewife.

In a statement explaining her reasons for leaving the stage, Lulu
mentioned her concern over people's increasing superstition. (Superstition refers to irrational belief, or attitudes that are not in keeping
with the known laws of science.)

She said, "I had become burdened with the idea of the vast
amount of superstition and delusion in the public mind concerning
the 'Power.' " She added, "As my fame grew, the superstition of the
people grew, and the burden grew likewise." She went on to say,
"I knew the Spiritualists everywhere were pointing to me as the mighty
'Medium,' though I always disclaimed such an appellation."

Still later, Lulu confessed how she had accomplished her wonders. Her original poltergeist-type effects were simply tricks. For example, like Margaret Fox, Lulu was able to make rapping sounds
with her toes.

As to her "Great Unknown" power, Lulu described it as "deflected
force." This she said was simply "unrecognized mechanical principles
involving leverage and balance." She explained that these principles
caused force applied against her to deflect, or glance off. Sometimes
the deflected force would even "recoil on the user."

In his *Secrets of Magic: Ancient and Modern,* Walter Gibson
explains force deflection:

For example, if a man extends his hands at arms' length and tries to raise a window, keeping his arms horizontal, he will exert a great amount of strength with no result. But if he approaches the window as closely as possible, and pulls it straight up, the task becomes an easy one. On the first attempt much of his force is expended in the wrong direction, but on the second, all energy is exerted upward in the right direction.

He adds:

A bullet travelling at a high rate of speed, may be deflected by striking a thin surface at an angle. A stone rebounds from water when it hits the water at the proper angle. In a similar manner, the force used against the "Georgia Magnet" was deflected into useless effort.

In the illustration accompanying this chapter, one can see that as the men push *toward* the woman, a cleverly directed *upward* pressure by her would effectively deflect their strength. If they pushed hard enough, and if her deflection were sudden and caught them off guard, they might be sent tumbling—much to the amusement of the audience.

In fact, Lulu Hurst was not the first such performer to make use of force deflection, along with other physical principles and tricks. In 1846 a French girl, Angelique Cottin, became known briefly as the "Electric Girl" for performing such stunts.

And long after Lulu Hurst had passed into obscurity, several imitators came forth. "One of the cleverest of these," according to magician Harry Houdini, was Annie Abbott. Her posters even billed her as "The Little Georgia Magnet." "Can you lift her?" the posters asked. "Twenty men try it every night—& fail."

Annie Abbott took her act to England in 1891. Her opening performance in London was a big sensation. Unfortunately, according to Houdini, "The Magnet failed to attract after about forty-eight hours, for a keen-witted reporter discovered her methods and promptly published them." Thus, she too soon faded from view.

Such was the fate of the "human magnets," but their stories still provide a lesson in the triumph of science over ignorance and superstition. No doubt Lulu Hurst—who ultimately repented of her deceptions—would have been pleased.

Selected Sources

Edwards, Frank. "Little Lulu—The Georgia Wonder," in *Strange People* (New York: Signet, 1961), pp. 13–20.

Fort, Charles. *The Complete Books of Charles Fort* (New York: Dover: 1974), pp. 1032–34.

Gibson, Walter. "The Georgia Magnet," in *Secrets of Magic: Ancient and Modern* (New York: Grosset & Dunlap, 1967), pp. 61–62.

Houdini, Harry. *Miracle Mongers and their Methods* (Toronto: Coles, 1980), pp. 228–239.

Rogo, D. Scott. *The Poltergeist Experience* (New York: Penguin, 1979).

SEER EXTRAORDINAIRE

Evangeline Adams

Another female wonder-worker was Evangeline Adams. She was a seer—that is, one who supposedly sees into the future. It is said that she even foresaw her own death!

Evangeline Smith Adams was born in Jersey City, New Jersey, on February 8, 1868. Hers was a prominent, influential family, although her father died when she was only fifteen months old.

She was educated in Andover, Massachusetts, where there were various academies, as well as a religious seminary and a girls' school. Her playmates were the children of the various teachers and professors. In this intellectual climate, all sorts of imaginative ideas—even frivolous notions—were tolerated.

During an illness, Evangeline's doctor became aware of her "unusual ideas." He suggested she see another doctor, a Boston University professor named J. Herbert Smith, who was also interested in the unusual. Smith believed in the ancient superstition called astrology.

Astrology is a means of fortune-telling. Those who believe in it claim it is a science by which a person's character, as well as his or her future, can be learned from the stars and planets. Depending on when one is born, a person supposedly comes under one of twelve astrological "signs." They are listed below, along with the main personality traits attributed to them (according to Miss Adams's own writings):

Date of Birth	Sign (and Symbol)	Traits
1. Mar. 22–Apr. 20	Aries (Ram)	ambitious, idealistic, high-spirited, generous
2. Apr. 21–May 21	Taurus (Bull)	home-loving, usually calm, fond of creature comforts
3. May 22–June 21	Gemini (Twins)	brilliant, changeable, charming
4. June 22–July 23	Cancer (Crab)	sensitive, nervous, home-loving
5. July 24–Aug. 23	Leo (Lion)	big, strong, regal (kingly)
6. Aug. 24–Sept. 23	Virgo (Virgin)	more intellectual than emotional, self-critical
7. Sept. 24–Oct. 23	Libra (Scales)	sociable, talented, frequently artistic
8. Oct. 24–Nov. 22	Scorpio (Scorpion)	passionate, whether temperamental or hard-working
9. Nov. 23–Dec. 22	Sagittarius (Archer)	frank, fearless, loyal, unselfish
10. Dec. 23–Jan. 20	Capricorn (Goat)	tenacious, able to overcome obstacles
11. Jan. 21–Feb. 19	Aquarius (Water-bearer)	interested in others, giving, loyal
12. Feb. 20–Mar. 21	Pisces (Fishes)	generous, popular, tend to be dreamers

In fact, however, astrologers like Miss Adams often assign contradictory traits to a sign. For example, we are told of Gemini people that they are "twins," but that "the two sides of their character war with each other." Or Taurians (Taurus people) are "agreeable" in their home life, yet we are warned: "It is never safe to wave the red flag in front of the bull!" Again, Libras are easy-going, yet "they have it in them to take a firm stand."

Also, similar characteristics are assigned to different signs. For instance, both Cancers and Taurians are said to be fond of the home. As well, Sagittarians (saj-uh-TARE-ee-uns) are "loyal," just like Aquarians. And both Sagittarians and Aries people are (at least according to Miss Adams) "idealists."

Actually, since the system of astrology was created, in ancient times, the earth's position in relation to the planets has shifted. Yet, most astrologers ignore this. Also, astrologers treat the "influences" of the planets as equal, although the planets are really different distances away from earth.

Putting aside these objections, one can still ask, as astrology critic Milbourne Christopher does:

> Why is someone born at a certain time, on a certain day, in a certain part of the world of a certain nature? Did the originators of astrology study the traits of millions of people and discover that all those born at a specific time had identical characteristics and futures? No! Nor has it been proven since that the early fictions are fact.

Nevertheless, Evangeline Adams soon found herself under the spell of astrology, especially after her teacher, Dr. Smith, told her she was a "born astrologer." To the shock of her family's upper-class friends, she opened an office in a Boston hotel. There she advised clients on matters of love, health, and business—based on what the "stars" supposedly "said."

Like other astrologers, she drew up an astrological chart for each client based on the time of his or her birth. Called a horoscope (which means "view of the hour"), the chart served as a basis for making predictions.

In 1899 Miss Adams, then in her thirties, claimed her own horoscope told her to seek her fortune in New York City. And just as she arrived at her hotel, she allegedly predicted immediate danger for its owner. The hotel supposedly burned the next day.

Many consider this proof that she could see the future. In fact, even if the story is true as it has been told, she only said that danger *might* occur the next day. She said nothing about what kind of danger it could be. Neither did she mention anything about the hotel or about a great fire.

This is the way many fortune-tellers work. They often make vague predictions. When these fail to come true, people forget about them, but people are impressed by even an occasional success. Also, there are usually many ways of interpreting a prediction or "prophecy" *after* some event has occurred.

Take, for example, the case of the hotel owner. Miss Adams would have seemed to have been correct if any of several things had occurred within a few days or even weeks. For instance, an injury, illness, or death could have happened to the man *or* to someone in his family. Or he could have suffered a financial blow (since he speculated on the stock market) or another misfortune. Even a near-accident would have seemed to fulfill the vague prophecy of "danger."

Actually, Miss Adams's alleged prophecy seems even further limited, since she did not foresee any misfortune for *herself,* yet most of her own belongings were destroyed in the fire!

Nevertheless, the publicity that reportedly resulted from her "correct" prediction enabled her to open an office in the Carnegie Hall Building. There she worked—and prospered—for the remainder of her life.

Then, in May 1914, came another problem for Miss Adams—which she again failed to foresee. She was arrested for violating a local law against fortune-telling. The *New York Times* reported that "Her reception room was crowded with fashionably dressed women" when a city detective "interrupted her work."

According to the authors of *The Book of Predictions,* "No doubt the judge was surprised when, instead of a gypsy with a crystal ball, a stout, strong-jawed, homely woman who looked and dressed like a practical, successful businesswoman walked into his courtroom."

The judge permitted Miss Adams to explain the principles of her "science." He showed interest in how a horoscope was drawn up. Then he gave her the time and place of birth of someone— he did not say whom—and waited while she consulted various tables. After she filled in the chart, she gave an analysis of the person. Supposedly, the judge was so impressed with the analysis, which seemed to correctly describe his son, that he dismissed the case.

Believers in astrology consider that Miss Adams thus "proved" the validity of the "science." However, an experiment conducted in more recent times shows how easy it can be to fit a personality description to anyone.

Psychologists at the University of Kansas told a group of people that they were each receiving their very own *personal* reading. However, unknown to these people, the psychologists had written only *one* personality sketch—a very generalized one. This "reading" was the one each person received. Yet, when asked to rate how well it described them, most of the people thought it was very accurate!

Nevertheless, Miss Adams's fame spread even more widely. It became a fad to consult her. In later years she would never tire of boasting about the famous people who came to her for advice: the early movie star, Mary Pickford; the popular singer, Enrico Caruso; the noted financier, J. Pierpont Morgan; and many others. She called the chair that faced her desk the "Seat of the Mighty" because of the great figures who had sat in it.

The visits of such famous people were good for Miss Adams's business. Many ordinary people were impressed. Such notables seemed to lend credibility to Miss Adams's "scientific" fortune-telling. Actually, all their visits really demonstrated is that famous people can be just as superstitious (and at least as interested in themselves) as anyone else.

In 1923, in her midfifties, Miss Adams finally married. She became Mrs. George E. Jordan, Jr., but continued to use her maiden name in connection with her astrology business.

She was not only famous now, but wealthy too. And both her wealth and fame increased. She began to write books that promoted astrology. She made personal appearances. Also, for the last two and a half years of her life she conducted a radio program on astrology. Three times a week, she gave advice and made predictions to many thousands of listeners.

It seemed that nearly everyone wanted to be told something about themselves. They flooded Miss Adams's mail with letters and postcards. In just one month, she received some 150,000 written requests for horoscopes.

Her prophecies about world events earned her the name "America's female Nostradamus." Nostradamus (NO-struh-DAH-mus) was a famous French astrologer and seer of the sixteenth century. The comparison seems appropriate when we look at the prophecies of each. For instance, consider this one of Nostradamus (who wrote all of his prophecies in verse):

> An Emperor shall be born near Italy,
> Who shall cost the Empire most highly.
> They shall say, from those around him he gathers,
> That he is less a prince than a butcher.

Many people have thought that this predicted the coming of Adolph Hitler, the ruthless German leader who brought on World War II. But it is so vague in its wording—"near Italy," for example— that others have thought it referred to the earlier French conqueror, Napoleon. Still others have thought it made reference to Ferdinand II, the Holy Roman Emperor who reigned from 1619 to 1637.

According to *The Book of Predictions,* "One of Evangeline's most famous predictions was made in 1931, when she prophesied that the U.S. would be involved in a war in 11 years." What she actually said was that there was a particular planetary situation (the planet Uranus being in "the sign Gemini") that occurs at long intervals. It occurred, she says, in 1776 and America fought the Revolutionary War. It occurred again in 1860 and the Civil War took place. She then added, "In 1942, Uranus again enters the sign Gemini—" but she did not finish the sentence, merely letting the suggestion speak for itself.

However, Miss Adams was not really playing fair with her historic dates. Battles in the war with England took place *the year before* the Declaration of Independence was signed. And the Civil War began not in 1860 but *the following year,* when the Confederates fired on Fort Sumter on April 12, 1861. And it was in 1941—not 1942—that America entered World War II.

Miss Adams also failed to discuss the numerous other wars that occurred between the ones she did mention: the War of 1812, the Black Hawk War, the Mexican War, the Spanish American War, and World War I—just to name a few.

But what about the claim that she predicted her own death, which occurred on November 10, 1932? Even if the story is true, Miss Adams, ill of heart disease, had merely announced that she would die before the year's end. Many seriously ill people know—or guess—that they have only months or even weeks to live.

Actually, however, according to a popular book on astrology, there is no proof that she made such a prediction. There is merely a *claim* that that was so, which a friend of hers made *after* her death. The book refers to the claim as providing a "touch of myth."

The occasional lucky guess, some vague statements that are open to various interpretations, a bit of fudging of the evidence—take these away and what is left of Evangeline Adams's supposed power to see the future? Apparently only as much ability as you or I have!

Selected Sources

Adams, Evangeline. *Astrology for Everyone* (New York: New Home Library, 1931).

Christopher, Milbourne. *ESP, Seers & Psychics* (New York: Thomas Y. Crowell, 1970), pp. 101–114.

MacNeice, Louis. *Astrology* (Garden City, N.Y.: Doubleday, 1964), pp. 196–198.

The National Cyclopedia of American Biography, vol. 25 (New York: James T. White & Co., 1936), p. 201.

Wallechinsky, David, Amy Wallace, and Irving Wallace. *The Book of Prediction* (New York: Bantam, 1981), pp. 363–366.

"THE MAN WHO WALKED THROUGH WALLS"

Harry Houdini

Harry Houdini was one of the world's greatest wonder-workers. He could apparently escape from any kind of restraint, seeming merely to shrug off handcuffs, shackles, chains with padlocks, even straitjackets. Neither a locked safe nor a jail cell could hold him. As he demonstrated many times, while under the watchful eyes of several observers, he could even walk through a solid brick wall!

His real name was Ehrich Weiss. The son of a Jewish rabbi, he was born March 24, 1874, in Budapest, Hungary. Until later in life, however, he believed he had been born in Appleton, Wisconsin, where he grew up.

Influenced at the age of nine by circus magicians and a traveling English conjurer named Dr. Lynn, Ehrich realized what he wanted to be when he grew up. He began to study books on magic and to practice sleight-of-hand tricks. His first audience was his little brother Theo, nicknamed "Dash." Soon he was giving neighborhood magic shows—first in Appleton, then in New York where Rabbi Weiss later moved his family.

About the age of sixteen, Ehrich read the *Memoirs of Robert-Houdin* (*see p. 19*). He decided to add an *i* to that magician's name, thinking it would mean "like Houdin." His mother having called him Ehrie, he took a similar sounding name that also began with an *H*, and so Ehrich Weiss became Harry Houdini (hoo-DEE-nee).

Briefly, he and Dash—calling themselves "The Brothers Houdini"—performed a double magic act, touring the Midwest. They performed in schools, music halls, traveling circuses and carnivals, and anywhere else they could. When they reached Chicago, in 1893, the World's Fair was in progress, and the brothers entertained in a sideshow there.

The following year, Harry met his future wife, Beatrice ("Bess") Rahner, at Coney Island. After only a month's courtship, they married. She then replaced Dash in the magic act.

The Houdinis performed on the vaudeville (VAWD-ville) circuit. This featured variety shows hired or "booked," in the lingo of the profession, not just for one performance hall, but for several. Each would be played in turn. Thus, a contract would provide many weeks of work.

The Houdinis also worked for a season with Welsh Brothers' Circus, then performed with a traveling show called "The American Gaity Girls." For a time Houdini featured sleight-of-hand tricks and billed himself as "Harry Houdini, King of Cards."

He and Bess also performed an illusion (as magicians term any large stage trick). They called it "Metamorphosis," which means "change." In this trick, Houdini would be tied up in a cloth sack, then placed in a locked trunk that was bound with rope. Bess would draw a curtain around it, step behind the curtain, and clap her hands three times.

Almost instantly the curtains would be flung open again and Houdini, minus his suit coat, would step forward to take a bow.

Bess would then be found, tied in the sack inside the trunk and wearing her husband's coat!

A later biography, titled *The Great Houdini,* explained:

> Nobody ever examined the bag and noticed that it had been slit open at the bottom; nobody ever found the concealed escape panel in the trunk. The speed with which the Houdinis performed made the transformation appear truly unbelievable and beyond explanation.

Harry also experimented with a handcuff release act, that is, escaping from a pair of handcuffs. It did not go over well, even when detectives brought their own, obviously unfaked, cuffs and Houdini easily shed them. The fact that he had to step from view for a brief time, while he took a piece of wire and picked open the lock, was something less than exciting.

Eventually he would learn that what he needed was *showmanship*—being able to make his act dramatically effective. He found ways to fill his escapes with suspense so that the audience became involved. Therefore, when he succeeded, they shared in his triumph.

In the meantime Houdini was learning to pick all kinds of locks. He discovered how to escape from a straitjacket. In first one city and then another, he challenged the police to handcuff him and lock him in a jail cell. Each time he escaped quickly. Being able to examine the cells beforehand, plus his knowledge of locks, gave him the advantage he needed.

When he found that people suspected he was using a lock pick or even a master key, he began to insist that he be stripped of his clothes and searched. He knew that his thick, curly hair was an excellent place to hide a small piece of wire!

At one time, down on their luck, the Houdinis did something they were later ashamed of. They became "spiritualists," putting on a show in which they pretended to communicate with spirits of the dead.

Lights in the theater would be extinguished. The "spirits" would ring bells, write messages on a slate, and perform other demonstrations that supposedly indicated their existence. To demonstrate that he was unable to produce the phenomena himself, Houdini would have himself tied and locked in a cabinet on stage. He, of course, used his special skill at escape to secretly free himself. Then in the dark he rang the bell and created the other effects.

The couple were glad when they soon found honest employment again. They knew it was one thing to deceive people for amusement in the way magicians do, but it was quite another to deceitfully encourage superstition and belief in the supernatural.

Eventually the Houdinis were rewarded by being booked on an important entertainment tour known as the Orpheum circuit. As "The Handcuff King," Houdini was a hit.

To publicize his act, as soon as they arrived in a new city Houdini issued his challenge to the local police chief to attempt to imprison or otherwise restrain him. For example, in San Francisco he freed himself from a dozen heavy manacles and fetters (strong handcuff-like restraints). His success meant a good crowd at the theater the following evening. But after the tour, the young performers again found themselves on hard times. In the spring of 1900, Houdini decided to take a big gamble. He determined to take their act to Europe where there were many important theaters.

At first ignored, the couple scored a big success when Houdini escaped from handcuffs at Britain's famous Scotland Yard. They promptly obtained a booking at London's Alhambra theatre, and from there their fame rose quickly.

They traveled throughout Europe. Houdini wriggled out of a straitjacket and threw off manacles and leg-irons in Germany. In Russia, he escaped from an armored prison van. In Holland, he was tied to the arm of a windmill, but it accidentally broke before he could effect his escape. Nevertheless, the publicity reached America.

When he returned to his home country, he was a star. For the next twenty years, his career was a string of sensational successes.

In Washington, Houdini escaped from the federal prison cell that had held President Garfield's assassin. He not only left his own cell, but he unlocked the other cells and switched the prisoners about, before relocking the doors.

Boston police waited twenty minutes for Houdini to escape from their jail. Just as they were about to congratulate themselves for finally restraining the famous magician, Houdini telephoned them from the Keith theater, a few minutes' drive away.

Houdini began to devise ever more unique and challenging escapes. Hanging upside down many stories above city streets, he performed his straitjacket escape, tossing the jacket to enthusiastic crowds below.

Handcuffed and placed inside a wooden packing box that was then nailed shut, chained, and lowered into a river, the elusive entertainer soon swam free. Huge crowds lining the river bank applauded wildly.

He escaped from a padlocked canvas mail sack, from a giant milk can, from safes and vaults, from a water-filled glass cabinet, and from a paper bag. Of course, anyone could escape from that, but Houdini had the bag tied with rope and the knots sealed with wax. He escaped without disturbing the seals or tearing the bag.

How did Houdini manage such daring feats? In being tied up or placed in a straitjacket, he took a deep breath and also expanded his muscles. Therefore, when he relaxed, the restraints did not fit so tightly, giving him an advantage. His superior knowledge of locks, as well as careful study and planning, also served him well.

To escape from safes, Houdini took advantage of the fact that they were made to keep burglars out, not to lock magicians in! Typically, they had a plate on the inside of the door that could be removed and so provide access to the locking mechanism. A concealed screwdriver and the proper knowledge were all that the great escapologist needed to free himself.

Houdini also had a sort of "secret weapon" that enabled him to accomplish many wonders. This was an assistant named James Collins, who was a master mechanic and craftsman. Collins was the unsung hero behind many of Houdini's successes.

For example, consider the packing-box escape. Although the wooden box appeared quite ordinary, Collins had transformed one end into a secret panel that Houdini could open from the inside.

To protect Houdini, Collins made sure that the box did not

go into the water too soon. He waited for Houdini's signal that he had shed his manacles or other shackles; then Collins had the box lowered into the river. All Houdini had to do was hold his breath until the box sank from view, then open the panel and swim free.

Many other confining devices and restraints were similarly "gimmicked" (altered in a trick fashion) to permit the magician's release. But not the paper bag. Houdini's method there was ingenious.

Tied in the bag, which was hidden from the audience's view behind a screen, Houdini produced a sharp blade. He made a small slit near the top of the bag and cut the cord. Stepping out of the bag he then repaired the damage, making everything look as before. He used a duplicate cord, which he had concealed by winding it around his body underneath his clothes. Of course, he also had the necessary materials with which to duplicate the seals, and he made sure that a seal covered the slit he had made.

As a result of such seemingly magical escapes, some superstitious people thought that Houdini could "dematerialize" his body. That is, they believed he could transform it in such a way that it could pass through solid barriers. In fact, with the trick, "Walking through a Brick Wall," he seemed to demonstrate just such a power.

To prove that a trapdoor was not used, a carpet would be placed on the stage floor. Then a section of solid brick wall, mounted on a platform with wheels, would be rolled to the center of the carpet. On each side of the wall a small, threefold screen was placed in such a way as to hide him from view. Houdini stepped behind one of these, while a number of people from the audience stood on all sides, watching from every direction.

Houdini now waved his arms to signal that he was still behind the screen. But after a few moments he would walk out from behind the screen on the opposite side! He had apparently passed through a solid wall!

The secret lay in the fact that—despite the carpet—a trap door *was* used. When it was opened secretly from below, the carpet sagged with the weight of Houdini's body, permitting just enough space for him to worm his way under the wall to the other side.

Houdini performed other magical illusions—such as causing an elephant to vanish on stage—and was engaged in many other activities as well. For example, he wrote several books. He invented a device that allowed a deep-sea diver to escape from his weighty suit in an emergency. And he was the first person to make a sustained airplane flight in Australia.

Houdini also made a number of films. These were serials, that is, films shown in weekly segments. At the end of each, Houdini would be in a perilous situation, only to escape from it in the next episode.

After his mother died in 1913, Houdini—who had long disbelieved in Spiritualism—became its foe. He seemed to take the claims that people could communicate with the dead as a personal insult. Because he had briefly practiced spiritualistic tricks himself, he knew how the fake mediums worked. He determined to expose their fraud publicly.

Wearing a disguise so he would not be recognized, Houdini began to visit their séances. In the dark he would grab the fake ghosts or otherwise interfere with the alleged spirit phenomena. He also gave public demonstrations that revealed how the tricks were done.

Houdini's own death came in 1926. While in Canada, he had allowed a young man to punch him in the stomach to prove what good shape he was in. Unfortunately, the blow ruptured Houdini's appendix.

Feverish and in pain, he nevertheless went on to complete a big stage show in Detroit so he would not disappoint those with tickets. Then he collapsed on stage as the curtains were drawn.

Because there were no antibiotics at that time (penicillin had not yet been developed), an infection set in, and Houdini died in a Detroit hospital. Fittingly, his end came on October 31—Halloween.

He was buried in a bronze coffin that he had bought with the intention of using it for an escape. His head rested on a bundle of his mother's letters. Over his coffin, a fellow magician ceremoniously broke a magic wand.

Soon after he was laid to rest, Spiritualist mediums claimed to have contacted Houdini's spirit. One, Arthur Ford, held séances with Bess in which he revealed parts of a message she and Houdini had arranged between them.

It was learned later, however, that Ford was a fake who secretly investigated people, learning facts from their friends, newspaper articles, and other sources. Then he revealed them as if they had come from the "spirit world."

Although first impressed with Ford's séances, Mrs. Houdini later concluded that her husband had not contacted her. For years, she kept an "eternal light" by a large photograph of Houdini, and each October 31 she would sit quietly to await any message. After ten years, she said: "Houdini hasn't come. I don't believe he will come." Sadly, she reached to the light by his portrait and turned it off.

Selected Sources

Christopher, Milbourne. *Houdini The Untold Story* (London: Cassell, 1969).

Gibson, Walter B. *Houdini's Escapes and Magic* (New York: Blue Ribbon Books, 1930).

Gresham, William Lindsay. *Houdini: The Man Who Walked Through Walls* (New York: Holt, 1959).

Williams, Beryl, and Samuel Epstein. *The Great Houdini* (New York: Scholastic Book Services, 1951).

THE X-RAY VIEWER

Joaquin Argamasilla

He was a young Spaniard who had the apparent power of "X-ray vision." This enabled him to see through metal, he claimed, even though blindfolded. As seeming proof, he could tell the time at which a watch was set, although its metal case was closed. And he could read what was written on a slip of paper, while it was kept in a padlocked box. The great Houdini called him a "phenomenal mystifier."

His name was Joaquin (wah-KEEN) Maria Argamasilla (ar-gam-uh-SEEL-yuh). He was born about 1905 in Madrid, the son of the Marquis (mar-KEY) de Santa Clara.

Little else is known about his background, but in 1924, at the age of nineteen, he appeared in the United States, making claim to supernormal vision. He was accompanied by a promoter, who also acted as interpreter since the Spaniard did not speak English.

Argamasilla brought with him letters attesting to his special powers. These came from noted scientists in Spain as well as Europe—including a Nobel prize winner from France. The letters claimed that the Spaniard had been tested and had proved to the scientists' satisfaction that he could actually see through metal—provided it was unpainted.

Now, the Spanish wonder-worker was not the first person who could apparently see while blindfolded. We recall the "second sight" act that Robert-Houdin performed with his young son. The lad did not actually see, but appeared to because of information his father secretly gave him. Thus, he could tell whether an object that he was asked to name was a watch, a comb, a coin, or another item.

Another who could evidently see while blindfolded was an entertainer named Washington Irving Bishop (1856–1889). He performed "mind reading" and similar wonders. One of his most sensational feats was an amazing carriage drive.

For this stunt, Bishop would blindfold himself, grasp the horses' reins, and set off at a brisk pace through city streets. While startled passersby stared in disbelief, other carriage drivers pulled aside to allow the magician to pass.

Bishop's feat has been widely imitated, although in different versions. "Newmann the Great" of Minneapolis was another who did the "blindfold drive" using a carriage. In recent times, the basic stunt has been performed with the entertainer driving an automobile. Still other performers have done the blindfold drive using a bicycle.

Yet another magical blindfold effect involves the supposed ability to "see" by means of one's skin. Typically, the subject's eyes are bandaged, and he or she identifies colors or reads newspaper headlines by merely passing the fingertips over them.

How are such feats possible? Well, the performer *does* actually manage to see. An ordinary blindfold does not prevent someone from peeking down the nose. By tilting the head back slightly, it is thus possible to see whatever is at one's fingertips.

There are also special, trick blindfolds that either restrict vision or permit it, as desired. A person who doesn't know the trick and wears one of these cannot see, but a magician sees just as before.

And there are even more elaborate forms of blindfold trickery.

Today's magician may be able to drive a car or perform a similar feat even with his eyes covered with wads of cotton, bandaged with adhesive tape, and bound with a cloth blindfold, and with his head then covered by a doubly thick black cloth sack!

Or consider this description of a "Master Blindfold Act" from a recent magicians' supply catalog:

> In this master method, a *genuine, unprepared,* black velvet blindfold is used and is tied around the performer's eyes by a committee. Cotton may be stuffed up under the blindfold and also above it, if so desired. (Emphasis added.)

The advertisement continues:

> Still, the performer is able to walk about freely and perform hundreds of tests as well as the complete routined act as supplied. Partial list of the act includes: The Dart and Board Test, The William Tell Sketch, Locating a Marked Coin, Blackboard and Chalk, Locating a Lost Article . . . and more.

(How is this done, you ask? As smart-alec magicians who do not wish to reveal their secrets are fond of replying, "Very *well,* thank you!")

But, you might point out, Argamasilla was not just blindfolded. Whatever he was to view was also covered with metal. How could he possibly succeed unless he really did have X-ray vision?

Houdini asked himself the same question. He began an investigation of the Spaniard and his methods. As Houdini would later write:

> It should be noted that Argamasilla always chooses a position with light behind himself, and such that observers are always *in front,* facing him. He very adroitly guards against observers being at his side or behind himself.

Houdini had several sessions with Argamasilla. On one of these he watched the young man place his left hand to his forehead as if in concentration. Houdini noticed, however, that in so doing, he very slightly raised the blindfold. In this way, Houdini noticed, he was able "to improve his downward line of vision."

One session was held at the office of the Newspaper Feature Syndicate in New York City. At this time, Houdini took the opportunity of sneaking behind the performer so that he could peer over his left shoulder. From this vantage point he learned the secret to the watch trick.

Here is what Argamasilla did. After the watch was set at a certain time, it was handed to him in a face-up position. He held it between his index finger and thumb at about the height of his chin.

Then he lowered his hand with a sweep, at the same time using his thumb to slightly open the watch case. His fingers concealed the little movement of the thumb and case, and the large sweeping movement diverted attention from the smaller movement. Magicians often distract the attention of observers this way; they call it "misdirection."

Houdini said the watch was only opened "a trifle"—about half an inch or so. Yet it was enough to permit the Spaniard to make a quick downward glance from beneath the blindfold.

Then the performer added a clever touch. Having noted the time at which the watch had been set, he would now briefly delay starting it. He would raise and lower the watch, as if bringing it into focus for his X-ray vision. This was, said Houdini, "simply acting." These added movements also provided misdirection so that no one would notice the small movement of closing the watch case.

Of course, the Spaniard had to allow for the lapse of time. Suppose the correct time, when he secretly glimpsed the face of the watch, was ten minutes after nine. If he stalled for approximately two minutes, he then announced the time as 9:12. As Houdini explained, ". . . though he might be thirty seconds out of the way, it is not of sufficient importance to note."

Although Houdini now knew the secret to the watch feat, he went one step further. He handed Argamasilla a watch that, he explained, was "tricky to open." As a result, the wonder-worker's supposed power of X-ray vision failed him, and he was unable to tell the time by that particular watch.

Houdini liked Argamasilla's watch trick enough to use it himself. He said: "Since witnessing his performance I have presented the watch trick and so far no one has been able to detect the movement unless knowing, before-hand, the trick of opening and closing the watch."

Argamasilla's other feat, reading a printed card or a written note locked inside a metal box, was also a trick. The Spaniard had two different boxes, and these were constructed in a special way to help make the trick work. Although each box did lock, its lid could still be raised a fraction of an inch. Light shining over his shoulder allowed him to peer into the narrow opening and read the writing or printing.

Again, to test Argamasilla, Houdini offered him three boxes of his own. One, which could be peeked into, Argamasilla readily accepted and successfully used to demonstrate his alleged power of X-ray viewing. Two other boxes, which had tight lids, were rejected by the Spaniard.

Therefore, his acceptance of the one and rejection of the others gave further proof that he was peeking in order to actually see what was in the boxes. Otherwise, the tightness of the lid should have nothing whatever to do with the ability to see through metal.

Why did Argamasilla insist that any boxes used were to be unpainted? Probably this was just part of the overall pretense, a means of making his pretended ability seem more limited and therefore more real. Of course, it also served as an excuse for him to reject many common boxes in favor of his own containers.

The fact that Argamasilla fooled famous scientists with his simple tricks should not be surprising. No matter how intelligent scientists are, unless they have knowledge of magic tricks they can easily be deceived by a clever person.

This is especially true if the deceiver is skilled, is a good actor, and seems honest. Argamasilla was all of these. Houdini said his handling of the watch "was so innocently done as to ward off suspicion." He added, "This man is a very clever manipulator, and he acts his part in such manner as to insure misdirection."

In a booklet that also attacked the claims of Spiritualists, Houdini revealed Argamasilla's secrets. Houdini explained in detail how each trick was done, complete with drawings.

Thus discredited, Argamasilla soon faded from view. His career as a dishonest wonder-worker had been derailed by the investigative work of an honest one.

Selected Sources

Abbott's Catalog 23 (Colon, Mich.: Abbott's Magic Manufacturing Co., 1987), p. 342.

Christopher, Milbourne. *Houdini: The Untold Story* (London: Cassell, 1969).

Gibson, Walter B., and Morris N. Young. eds. *Houdini on Magic* (New York: Dover, 1953), pp. 248–257.

Hay, Henry. *Cyclopedia of Magic* (Washington Square: David McKay Co., 1949), pp. 27–29.

MASTER MIND READER

Joseph Dunninger

The "Amazing Dunninger" astonished people by appearing to know their innermost thoughts. So convincing were his demonstrations that he seemed entitled to bill himself as "The Man with the Miracle Mind."

Joseph Dunninger was born in New York City, April 28, 1892 (although some sources say 1896). His parents were Nicholas and Caroline (Gottchalk) Dunninger.

Joe was what is known as a child prodigy—someone with exceptional talent. While still in grade school he began to put on magic shows—inspired, he later said, by having seen a performance of the great magician Harry Kellar. He soon became known as "The Child Wonder Magician."

By the age of sixteen, he was giving nightly shows at a local performance hall. This lasted for some sixty-five weeks, making his the longest running act in that establishment's history.

Like many parents before and since, Joe's mother did not think a magician's life was suitable for her son. Instead, she desired a nice respectable business career for him. So to try to please her, and yet be true to his own wishes, he took a second, daytime job at Wanamaker's, a New York department store.

His success at magic soon, however, overcame his mother's opposition. While still a teenager, he set out—like Houdini before him—on the vaudeville circuits. By the age of twenty he was a "stage headliner"—that is, a performer advertised as a main attraction.

Years later, in his old age, Dunninger explained:

> One reason for my rapid success was that I varied my performances instead of limiting myself to one field. This enabled me to change my program and make new tours over the same vaudeville circuits, or give repeat shows at clubs and theaters where I had already appeared.
>
> This was at variance with the usual pattern, as magicians of those days liked to specialize in certain fields. There were Card Kings, Coin Kings, Silk Kings, and Escape Kings. One performer even put on an entire act using only watches and clocks.

At the height of his vaudeville appearances, his act was extravagantly billed as "Dunninger, the Master Mind of Mystery and His Company of Temple Dancers from the Far East . . . Producing a Beautiful Girl from Thin Air . . . The Flight of the Night Rider . . . Is It Dunninger or Is It Not? . . . The Balloon that Floats Out Over the Audience and Vanishes . . . And Many Other Baffling Features."

Eventually, however, he put aside his magic act to become a "mentalist"—a magician who supposedly reads minds. Dunninger eliminated elaborate props, assistants, and fanfare, appearing alone with such simple items as a deck of cards or a slate and chalk.

Dunninger differed from other so-called mind readers in an important respect. He claimed "neither supernatural nor supernormal powers." Yet he certainly seemed to have such powers.

For instance, during his stage shows, Dunninger would answer questions from the audience, even though they had been written out of his sight and then sealed in envelopes.

At other times, Dunninger would *predict* what choice someone would make—for instance, what playing card he or she would select from a shuffled deck.

Another example of Dunninger's apparent power was demonstrated at a meeting with Thomas Edison, the great inventor. While Edison *thought* of the word "osmium" (the name of a heavy metallic element), Dunninger slowly wrote it, letter by letter, on a pad of paper. Interestingly enough, Dunninger insisted that, at that time, he was unfamiliar with the word.

While these feats seem impressive and appear to prove that Dunninger could indeed read minds, they actually were accomplished either by trickery or through the use of simple principles.

For example, there are literally dozens of ways to read what someone else has written. One such way is the so-called "one ahead" principle.

In this method, the mind reader makes a secret arrangement with one member of the audience before the show. They agree on what question the person is to write. Let's say it will be, "Who was our first president?"

Now the magician collects the envelopes from the audience and places the one from the secret helper on the bottom. Then he or she takes one of the other envelopes and, pretending to use psychic power, says: "The answer to this person's question is George Washington."

Tearing the envelope open the mentalist pretends to verify what was written, but is actually reading *someone else's question!*

Now it's time to repeat the trick. Holding up the second envelope, the mentalist answers the question just learned. By tearing open this envelope the next question is revealed, and so on, until all the envelopes have been gone through.

Of course, not knowing an answer is all right. The mentalist frankly admits it, but makes sure the audience knows that at least the question has been read correctly. That is all that is necessary to appear to be a genuine mind reader.

In making predictions, again Dunninger could use a variety of methods. For example, with playing cards, he could simply cause the person to choose the card that had been predicted. The simplest way to do this is to have a special trick deck in which there are not fifty-two *different* cards but rather fifty-two of the *same* card: say queen of diamonds.

All one does is write the prediction, "queen of diamonds," on a slip of paper, fold it, and place it on the table. After the cards are shuffled, the person is asked to select one. Naturally he or she selects a queen of diamonds. The performer then opens the slip of paper to show that the "prediction" came true.

In apparently reading Thomas Edison's mind, Dunninger used a special principle rather than a trick. He began by approaching the unknown word one letter at a time.

Then, while holding the great inventor's wrist, Dunninger, slowly recited the alphabet. This he did out loud at first, then, having established a pace for the reciting, he continued silently.

Quite unintentionally, through his unconscious *reactions,* Edison signaled that "O" was the correct first letter. Such reactions might consist of muscular impulse, nervous tension, or even facial expressions or some other revealing cue.

Dunninger did not explain the exact nature of the reaction in Edison's case, except to say, "I could literally sense the approach of each letter, so that when I reached it, it was like a peak. . . ." In other words, by holding Edison's wrist, Dunninger was sensing his physical reactions, rather like a lie detector would have done.

By going through the alphabet for each letter in turn, Dunninger determined that Edison was thinking of O-S-M-I-U-M.

Some of Dunninger's methods were quite complicated. Others were deceptively simple. Sometimes he simply took a guess, knowing that he could scarcely lose: If he was correct, he would appear to have phenomenal powers. But if he was wrong, he knew that his error would soon be forgotten.

On some occasions, Dunninger simply relied on human nature. Such was the case when he predicted the choices a magazine editor would make. On each of four slips of paper, the master mentalist wrote something. Then he asked the editor to name the following: a number from one to five, a color, an article of furniture, and a flower.

After the editor wrote down his choices, Dunninger revealed what he'd already written on his own slips of paper. The predictions exactly matched what the editor had written: "3—RED—CHAIR—ROSE." Dunninger seemed to have read the editor's thoughts even before he had had them!

The matter is seen to be quite simple, however, when the secret is told. As Dunninger himself explained, in his book *Dunninger's Secrets:*

> When these choices are analyzed, it becomes obvious that they should naturally spring to mind. The figure "3" represents the midpoint, or balance, between one and five. Red is the first color of the spectrum, or rainbow, and the first used in naming the colors of the American flag. A chair is the commonest article of furniture, and the editor was sitting on one when I handed him the pad. The rose is the predominant flower of song and story.

Not everyone will make the same four choices, of course. But even getting some of them correct will convince many people that ESP (extrasensory perception) has been demonstrated.

Dunninger knew that some people would not make the obvious choices. He called one such type of person a "second chooser," one likely to pick "4—BLUE—TABLE—ORCHID."

Another type was the "joker" who would pick "1½" as the number, "puce" for the color, and so on. Dunninger said: "Personally, I screen such characters beforehand, by learning something of their likes and dislikes, or sounding them out by working a test with a more susceptible person, and watching their reactions."

On September 12, 1943, Dunninger launched a radio show. According to one source, it "evoked wide popular enthusiasm." Later he had a television show, "Amazing Dunninger," which lasted until 1968.

From then until his death, Dunninger continued to write, as

he had for much of his professional career. He wrote several books of magic tricks, as well as books critical of fake phenomena such as Spiritualism. In 1928, for example, he published his *Dunninger-Houdini Spirit Exposés*.

Following the lead of his friend Houdini, Dunninger offered $10,000 to anyone who could produce any seemingly magical or mystical phenomena that he could not either duplicate or explain.

To mediums who claimed they could contact the dead, Dunninger had a special test. This was to correctly reproduce the words of a message that a friend had sent him before his death. The friend was Sir Arthur Conan Doyle, author of the Sherlock Holmes detective stories. No one ever succeeded in revealing the secret message or otherwise claiming Dunninger's $10,000.

Approaching his eighty-third birthday, Dunninger died on March 9, 1975, of Parkinson's disease (a nervous disease also known as "shaking palsy"). He was survived by his widow, Billie, and by two daughters and four grandchildren.

He was also survived by his reputation as a master mentalist. A guide to magic titled *The Magic Catalog* states he was "probably the greatest mentalist of all time," pointing out that when he died "he took the secrets of his greatest effects with him."

Selected Sources

Current Biography (New York: H. W. Wilson Co. 1944), pp. 183–185.

Doerflinger, William. *The Magic Catalog* (New York: Dutton, 1977), pp. 131–136.

Dunninger, Joseph, as told to Walter Gibson, *Dunninger's Secrets* (Secaucus, N.J.: Lyle Stuart, 1974).

"THE SLEEPING PROPHET"

Edgar Cayce

Edgar Cayce (pronounced KAY-see) was a seer, like Evangeline Adams (*see p. 43*), but he did not use astrology for making predictions. Rather, he went into a "sleeping" (trancelike) state in which he could supposedly view future events, as well as diagnose illnesses, even at a distance!

He was born in 1877 on a farm near Hopkinsville, Kentucky. He has been described as a "dreamy" child—one especially prone to fantasies. For example, he had imaginary playmates.

Edgar's schooling did not reach past the ninth grade, but he worked in a bookstore and read extensively. His approach to reading, however, was somewhat like that of a small child who, allowed to choose what he wants for supper, selects cake, pie, and candy.

Instead of scientific or scholarly books, young Cayce apparently read mostly about mystical subjects and quack medical practices. In other words, he chose pseudoscience (SUE-doe-science)—that is, imitation science—over genuine scientific studies.

Cayce became a photographer and operated a studio in Hopkinsville, where he met a man named Al Layne. Layne had wished to become a doctor but circumstances had prevented this. Instead he took cheap, mail-order courses in hypnotism (HIP-nuh-tiz-um) and osteopathy (oss-tee-OP-uh-thee).

Hypnotism, or the practice of hypnosis, involves attempting to influence people by making suggestions to them while they are in a state resembling sleep. Osteopathy is a quaint theory of healing that emphasizes "manipulation"—or special application of the healer's hands to joints, muscles, etc.

Cayce soon discovered that he was a good hypnotic subject—that he could even put himself into a trance. In this condition he gave people information about their health. He seemed able to diagnose illnesses and prescribe remedies for them.

A typical reading might go like this:

> Yes, we can see the body. The trouble we see is a partial paralysis of the vocal chords, due to nerve strain. This is a psychological condition producing physical effect. It may be removed by increasing the circulation to the affected parts by suggestion while in the unconscious condition.

Actually, this was a reading for Cayce's very first patient: himself. He had had a case of laryngitis that had resisted standard medical treatment. His self-cure is not too amazing, though. As just about everyone today knows, ailments that are "psychological," like Cayce's, may well respond favorably to positive "suggestion." The beneficial effects of hypnotism are widely acknowledged. Here is another Cayce reading:

> The condition in the body is quite different from what we have had before . . . from the head, pains along through the body from the second, fifth and sixth dorsals, and from the first and second lumbar . . . tie-ups here, and floating lesions, or lateral lesions, in the muscular and nerve fibers which supply the lower

end of the lung and the diaphragm . . . in conjunction with the sympathetic nerve of the solar plexus, coming in conjunction with the solar plexus at the end of the stomach. . . .

This gobbledygook language could describe any of a number of ailments. It was actually for a subject (Cayce's wife, in fact) who had tuberculosis.

Nevertheless, Cayce's apparent successes in the circle of those who knew him gained him notoriety. He became known locally as a sort of eccentric folk doctor.

Then on October 9, 1910, the *New York Times'* Sunday magazine ran an article headlined: "ILLITERATE MAN BECOMES A DOCTOR WHEN HYPNOTIZED—STRANGE POWER SHOWN BY EDGAR CAYCE PUZZLES PHYSICIANS."

The article began:

The medical fraternity of the country is taking a lively interest in the strange power said to be possessed by Edgar Cayce of Hopkinsville, Ky., to diagnose difficult diseases while in a semiconscious state, though he has not the slightest knowledge of medicine when not in this condition.

Note the exaggerations in the article, beginning with the first word of the headline. Cayce was far from "illiterate." And, in fact, his various diagnoses suggest he was influenced by osteopathy and other quaint theories of medicine, obtained from books and from his association with people like Layne. As one Cayce critic, Martin Gardner, observes:

Most of Cayce's early trances were given with the aid of an osteopath who asked him questions while he was asleep, and helped later in explaining the reading to the patient. There is abundant evidence that Cayce's early association with osteopaths and homeopaths had a major influence on the character of his readings. Over and over again he would find spinal lesions of one sort or another as the cause of an ailment and prescribe spinal manipulations for its cure.

In addition to osteopathic manipulations, Cayce prescribed electrical treatments, special diets, and various tonics and other remedies. For a leg sore, he recommended something called "oil of smoke." For a baby with convulsions he prescribed "peach-tree poultice." And for a priest with an epilepsylike condition, Cayce urged the use of "castor oil packs."

Cayce also prescribed castor oil for warts and blemishes, as well as other conditions. He offered several remedies for baldness. These included giving the scalp a rubbing with crude oil and "Listerine twice a week."

In addition, Cayce thought almonds could prevent cancer. To cure tuberculosis and other diseases he recommended ash from the wood of a bamboo tree. And, for an ailment called dropsy, Cayce prescribed "bedbug juice"!

If such silly treatments are easily dismissed, how could Cayce apparently diagnose people's illnesses from hundreds of miles away? Many people sent Cayce letters requesting his "medical" help.

In fact, today Cayce's followers point to thousands of case histories that are on file at the library of the Association for Research and Enlightenment. (The association is an institution that promotes belief in Cayce's alleged powers. It was founded by the sleeping prophet's son.)

Supposedly, the files show many accurate diagnoses of people who followed Cayce's advice and came to believe themselves cured. Many such people wrote testimonials to Cayce's seeming successes.

However, James Randi has studied the records of Cayce's supposedly medical readings. Randi found them full of "half truths" and "evasive and garbled language." As he explained:

> Cayce was fond of expressions like "I feel that . . ." and "perhaps"—qualifying words used to avoid positive declarations. It is a common tool in the psychic trade. Many of the letters he received—in fact, most—contained specific details about the illnesses for which readings were required, and there was nothing to stop Cayce from knowing the contents of the letters and presenting that information as if it were a divine revelation. To

one who has been through dozens of similar diagnoses, as I have, the methods are obvious. It is merely a specialized version of the "generalization" technique of fortune-tellers.

In fact, like Evangeline Adams, Cayce was arrested in New York on a charge of fortune-telling. He was acquitted, however, on the basis of religious freedom.

Over time, Cayce became more and more mystical. He began to believe in reincarnation (re-in-car-NAY-shun), the idea that people have lived previous lives in other bodies. He began to describe for his subjects the previous lives he imagined for them.

He also began to describe their "auras." (An aura is a supposed halolike field of energy that mystics believe everyone has.) Cayce claimed he could actually see auras and from them he could diagnose people's character and health.

In addition to medical readings, Cayce also made hundreds of financial forecasts, dream interpretations, mental and spiritual readings, readings concerning the home and marriage, and about a thousand miscellaneous readings.

Cayce's claims were never subjected to proper scientific testing. Dr. J. B. Rhine, the famous ESP researcher, was unimpressed with Cayce's claims, for example. A reading that Cayce gave for Dr. Rhine's daughter was quite inaccurate.

At times, Cayce was even more inaccurate. He provided diagnoses of subjects *who had died* since their letters had been sent! Unaware of the fact, Cayce simply rambled on in his usual fashion. For one, he prescribed an incredible mixture made from Indian turnip, wild ginseng, and other ingredients. As Randi says of Cayce's failure to know these patients were deceased, "Surely, dead is a very serious symptom, and should be detectable."

Eventually Cayce began to make Nostradamus-like predictions. These are not impressive. According to Steven Tyler, in his book *ESP and Psychic Power:* "With slight exception they were all made within a few years of the events coming to pass and at a time when many people, not in the least psychic, were saying the same things."

Tyler explains: "For instance, that the Depression would lift in 1933 was a prediction made in 1931 and expressed a view held by many economic analysts at that time." Apparently, Cayce was once again using things he had read about to give the impression he had special powers.

Sometimes his forecasts were even laughable. For instance, he predicted that Atlantis—the mythical sunken continent—would rise again in the late 1960s. It did not, of course. Nevertheless, before his death Cayce told numerous clients that in their previous lives they had been citizens of Atlantis. No doubt many believed him.

Cayce died in 1945, apparently without foreseeing his own end. According to his obituary, he had experienced doubts about the source of his psychic visions. Did they come from God, he wondered, or some less desirable source? As one writer, Owen Rachleff, says:

> Cayce's quandary points up the sincere confusion of many psychics and other occult practitioners. Not all of them, after all, are outright frauds as are the dime-a-dozen readers and advisors, the fly-by-night séance swindler, and the phony faith healers and medicine men. Nor are all of them of the more subtle variety, who carefully cover their tracks and stay within the law by ambiguous and relatively innocuous prophecies, read-ings, and assorted visions of a grandiose but legal formulation. This last type never advertises any more than he delivers, thus protecting himself from the accusation of criminal fraud. The fraudulent aspect of this subtle deceiver, however, is the fact that he *knowingly* employs outlandish and discredited systems of "magic," under the guise of viable truths.

Whatever may be the truth about Cayce's sincerity, one simple fact remains. Those who still insist that he had some special powers come from the ranks of Cayce's fellow mystics. The realm of modern medicine—with its X-rays, cardiographs, and similar diagnostic aids —shows no interest in the sleeping prophet.

Selected Sources

Gardner, Martin. *Fads & Fallacies in the Name of Science* (New York: Dover Publications, 1957), pp. 216–219.

Rachleff, Owen S. *The Occult Conceit* (Chicago: Cowles, 1971), pp. 145–146.

Randi, James. *Flim-Flam!* (Buffalo, N.Y.: Prometheus Books, 1982), pp. 189–195.

Tyler, Steven. *ESP and Psychic Power* (New York: Tower Publications, 1970), pp. 34–48.

PSYCHIC DETECTIVE

Peter Hurkos

Peter Hurkos closed his eyes and concentrated. The vision became clear: He knew who the murderer was! This appeared to be another triumph for Hurkos, "the man with the radar brain."

His real name was Pieter van der Hurk. He was born in Holland, in the city of Dordrecht (DOR-drekt), on May 21, 1911.

Unfortunately, there is little accurate information about his early life. That is because over the years he gave different tales about his background, and he frequently exaggerated. We must keep this in mind, therefore, as we proceed with our story.

Supposedly, Peter left school at age sixteen in order to become a merchant seaman. (That is, he worked on a boat that was engaged in commercial trade, as opposed to a navy ship.) This was mostly a winter job in which he kept records of the cargo and passengers.

On one trip home, in 1937, he married his sweetheart, Bea van der Berg. She and Peter soon had two children, a boy and a girl.

During summers Peter often helped his family with their painting business. Supposedly, one summer he had an accident. Maybe it was in 1941, although another version says 1943. Peter was helping his father paint a schoolhouse—or was it a German airplane hangar? (The Germans occupied Holland during World War II.) Again there are conflicting versions.

In any case, Peter claimed he fell from a ladder and hit his head. After recovering in a hospital, he supposedly discovered he had psychic ability. Specifically, he claimed that he could see beyond the normal range, viewing things at a distance or even peering into the future!

Hurkos stated that one of his earliest psychic visions concerned a fellow patient. (Whether the hospital was in Amsterdam or a different Dutch city, called The Hague, is yet another detail that changes from story to story.) The man, a British agent, was about to be released, and Hurkos "saw"—two days into the future—that the man would be killed. German secret police would shoot him down on a particular street, said the psychic.

Unfortunately, Hurkos later claimed, when he told this to the hospital staff, they didn't believe him. They thought the injury to his head had caused him to hallucinate—that is, to have a sort of fantasy dream. And so, on the predicted day and at the foreseen location, the agent was shot and killed—or so Peter Hurkos maintained.

In fact, though, the story doesn't check out. Some forty years later a Dutch skeptic named Hoebens (HO-binz) investigated the claim. By contacting those in charge of war records to see if a British agent had really met such a fate, Hoebens learned otherwise. An official reported that no such event was recorded, either for Amsterdam "or any other Dutch town." The official labeled the alleged occurrence "improbable."

Hurkos claimed that he worked with the Dutch underground during the war. It was made up of people who secretly banded together to resist the Nazi occupiers. Hurkos claimed that in his resistance work he performed many brave acts.

For example, he told a remarkable story about freeing one of his underground friends who had been arrested by the Germans. Hurkos claimed that he posed as a German officer, disguised in the appropriate uniform, and entered the German camp.

He told the Nazi soldiers that the prisoner was to be turned over to him to be taken to headquarters for questioning. Afraid his friend would recognize him and give him away, Hurkos immediately began beating him and calling him names. When his friend was unconscious from the blows, Hurkos had him loaded into a staff car, which he then drove to safety.

This was another story that the skeptical Hoebens investigated. Again, war files were checked, but there was no record of any such remarkable escape. Also, it was doubtful that the Dutchman's German speech could have been so perfect, so free of any telltale accent, that it would have fooled real Nazi soldiers.

Another Hurkos tale has him captured by the Germans near the end of the war. Supposedly, he was arrested for having forged papers in his possession and was sent to Buchenwald (BOO-ken-valt), a notorious German prison camp.

One would think that, if he actually had psychic powers as he claimed, those powers would have enabled him to elude his captors. Actually, the story of his arrest and imprisonment is just another one that does not check out.

Indeed, he gave a very different version to Norma Lee Browning, who wrote two biographies of Hurkos. The Dutchman told her that his arrest had been for illegally cutting firewood, and that he had been sent for punishment to a Dutch labor camp.

A final war-related story (another tale that Hurkos told Browning) alleges that the Dutch underground "hero" was honored after the war at Holland's Royal Palace. There, we are told, Queen Juliana herself presented Hurkos and his comrades each with a scroll and a gold medal.

Once again, though, investigation failed to prove that any such public ceremony took place. Neither was there any record of Hurkos's particular group of resistance fighters.

These apparently false stories help set the stage for judging Peter Hurkos's claims of psychic power. He stated that after the war he was unable to work at his previous jobs because his psychic visions were too distracting.

Like the master mentalist Dunninger (*see p. 69*), Hurkos was soon demonstrating his alleged psychic powers on stage. He probably began performing in a variety show in The Hague in 1946. He then embarked on a tour of Europe.

About this time he divorced his wife and married a Belgian beautician named Maria. They had several children. (The couple lived together for almost twenty years. Then Maria left him.) Hurkos also began calling himself "Dr. Hurkos," but he stopped after a time.

During Hurkos's European period he also began assisting police departments, not only in his native Holland, but in France, Germany, England, and elsewhere. Supposedly, Hurkos used his reputed powers to solve baffling crimes.

For example, consider his first case, which occurred in Holland in 1946. Hurkos reportedly used a psychic power called psychometry (sigh-KOM-uh-tree) to solve a murder. Psychometry is the alleged power of psychically obtaining information from some object.

In this case, we are told, Hurkos was brought a coat that had belonged to the murdered man. The victim had been a coal miner in the Limburg region and had been shot to death.

After handling the coat, Hurkos reportedly identified the killer— the miner's stepfather—and told police where they would find the murder weapon. The pistol, he stated, would be found on the roof of the victim's house.

The police discovered the pistol just where Hurkos said, and fingerprints on the gun proved the stepfather's guilt. Hurkos's power of psychometry seemed confirmed.

Hurkos's "masterpiece" was a case he claimed to have solved in 1951. Mysterious fires were being set in a Dutch town. Hurkos pointed to a seventeen-year-old boy, son of a well-to-do family. The police chief refused to believe the psychic's accusation until, under Hurkos's questions, the young arsonist confessed.

Such stories would seem to provide evidence of Hurkos's amazing powers—powers that eventually gained him fame as "the man with the radar brain." Unfortunately, however, as with his wartime tales, the truth of these accounts is typically quite different from the way the Dutch psychic represented them.

Reporters investigating the case of the murdered miner learned that the police contradicted the version of events as told by Hurkos. Actually, he had predicted the gun would be found in a little brook, not on the roof. The police searched the stream in vain, and it was much later that the pistol was discovered on the roof. It was done without any help from Hurkos.

As for the suspect, the police already had him in custody when Hurkos became involved in the case. So, the truth is that, except for telling the police what they already believed, Hurkos had been completely wrong!

A similar situation occurred in the case of the seventeen-year-old firebug. The boy had mental problems and had been suspected due to an earlier fire at his place of employment. In fact, far from being unwilling to believe the boy's guilt, the police had arrested him *the day before* Hurkos appeared on the scene. Once again, Hurkos distorted the facts to make it appear that he had psychic powers.

Some of Hurkos's alleged solutions had even simpler explanations. Take the case of a priest murdered in Amsterdam, for instance. Hurkos's solving of the case reportedly earned him a letter of commendation from the Pope. Investigation revealed, however, that no such murder had ever taken place!

In 1956 Hurkos came to the United States where he gave his psychic impressions to interested people, much as Evangeline Adams had done before. Hurkos's technique was to make many vague statements, some of which would doubtless prove successful. Hurkos also performed in various clubs as a mentalist, doing his Dunninger-like routine.

In 1964 Peter Hurkos was brought into a major American murder case, that of the so-called "Boston Strangler." Over an eighteen-month period, a killer had strangled eleven women to death. Bostonians became increasingly afraid, as the police grew more and more frustrated at being unable to solve the murders.

As it happened, however, Hurkos identified the wrong man, a shoe salesman who was completely innocent of the crimes. (The real killer later confessed.) As one detective said of Hurkos: "He did nothing. . . . He did not contribute one thing to the solution of the Boston Strangler murders."

Worse, Hurkos was himself soon arrested for impersonating an FBI agent! In his possession were guns and a collection of police badges. This was just the sort of stuff, said the critic, that was "ideal equipment for putting up the front necessary to obtain information about police matters." Hurkos convinced the judge in the case that the incident was a mistake, but he was later convicted and fined $1,000.

These events hurt Hurkos's reputation and it took him years to get over them. Then he married his third wife—a woman thirty-three years younger than himself. She gave him a new daughter and helped him restart his career.

In the late 1960s, Hurkos was able to collect $2,500 for a weekend's performance at Lake Tahoe and $10,000 for one week at a Los Angeles theater.

Over the next several years, he made pronouncements in a number of famous cases: a group of murders in Michigan; another group in Los Angeles (instigated by madman Charles Manson); the disappearance of union leader Jimmy Hoffa; the kidnaping of a teenage Palm Springs, California, boy; and others. But Hurkos was useless—or worse than useless—in each.

Hurkos claimed his powers had been tested and verified by scientists. In fact, Dr. J. B. Rhine at Duke University issued this denial: "Hurkos has *not* been investigated at the Duke laboratory and is not known to have given any such performance as those claimed in any university laboratory." Hurkos did undergo one series of tests performed by a skeptical scientist in Belgium. He failed.

In 1975 Hurkos unknowingly participated in a test that proved to be an embarrassment. On a TV program, he was given a shirt and other items that supposedly belonged to Jimmy Hoffa. Hurkos used his alleged power of psychometry to describe what he said were Hoffa's last days, his whereabouts, and so forth.

Then, at the end of the program it was revealed that none of the items had belonged to Hoffa! Instead, they had come from the

TV host's own closet! Outsmarted, Hurkos sat stunned as the program ended, then called the host bad names and stormed away.

One of Hurkos's last notorious activities was in 1987 when he appeared on the Geraldo Rivera TV show. There, Hurkos claimed that the United States Navy had employed him as an official psychic for many years. When challenged for proof after the show, however, Hurkos had none.

The following year, at the age of seventy-seven, Peter Hurkos died. His death came just four days after his birthday. Interestingly enough, he had once predicted that he would die on November 17, 1961. But, once again, his "radar brain" failed him.

Selected Sources

Archer, Fred. *Crime and the Psychic World* (New York: William Morrow, 1969), pp. 157–161.

Edwards, Frank. *Strange People* (New York: Signet, 1961), pp. 175–182.

Lyons, Arthur, and Marcello Truzzi. *The Blue Sense: Psychic Detectives and Crime* (New York: Mysterious Press, 1991), pp. 107–128.

Randi, James. *Flim-Flam!: Psychics, ESP, Unicorns and Other Delusions* (Buffalo: Prometheus Books, 1986), pp. 270–273.

A Note to Teachers

Like the author's previous children's book, *The Magic Detectives* (Prometheus 1989), *Wonder-workers!* can help teach young people valuable skills—such as reasoning ability and critical thinking—as well as foster appreciation of rational and scientific thinking over irrational thought and superstition. And, because it deals with various types of deception, it offers many opportunities for reinforcing such positive values as honesty and respect for others.

Some stories help dramatize and explain various principles of physics (such as thermal conductivity in "The Fire King," and force deflection in "The Human Magnet"), while others provide interesting sidelights on such topics as robots, stage magic, folk medicine, hypnotism, and more.

The stories can be used in a variety of ways. For example, they can constitute a basis for class discussion, provide subjects for writing essays, inspire various class projects, and so on.

Here are some specific suggestions for assignments:

1. Discuss with your classmates the ethical difference between the trickery of phony psychics and that of stage magicians.
2. Learn a few mind-reading tricks like Dunninger used and perform them for your classmates. (Remember that magicians do not reveal the secrets to their tricks.)
3. After some research in the library, report to your fellow students on some other famous wonder-worker.
4. Write an essay comparing two of the performers in *Wonder-*

workers!—say Houdini and Argamasilla. In what ways were they alike, and in what ways different?

5. Give a book report—either oral or written—on a book you've read that relates to one of the stories in *Wonder-workers!*

6. Assist a friend with his or her report or essay by drawing an illustration for it.

7. Devise an experiment to test the accuracy of the horoscopes that appear in your daily newspaper. (For example, copy down the twelve forecasts in scrambled order and—without identifying which is Aries, Virgo, etc.—give a copy to each person in your class, asking everyone to try to judge which is his or her own.)

8. Select one of the stories in *Wonder-workers!* and make a list of all the new words that you have learned from it. Write a definition of each in your own words.

9. Learn about some paranormal mystery ("haunted" house, UFO case, etc.) that has been solved. (*The Magic Detectives* is an ideal source for this.) Present the mystery to your fellow pupils, giving them some clues and encouraging them to solve it. Of course, be prepared to fully explain the solution at the end.

10. Using pantomime, briefly act out the role of one of the characters in *Wonder-workers!* Ask your classmates to guess who you are imitating.